This Book Belongs To

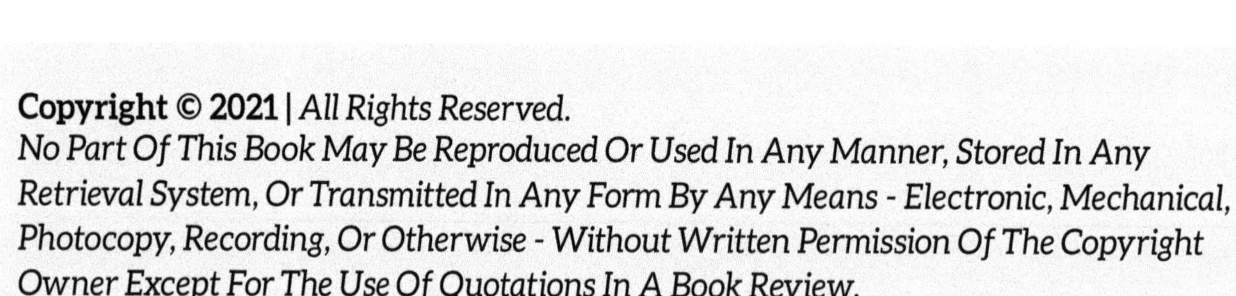

Trace The Letter Then Write Your Own.

A A A A A A A A A

a a a a a a a a a a a a

Trace The Letter Then Write Your Own.

B B B B B B B B B

b b b b b b b b b b b b

Trace The Letter Then Write Your Own.

C C C C C C C C C C

c c c c c c c c c c c c c c

Trace The Letter Then Write Your Own.

D D D D D D D D

d d d d d d d d d d d d

Trace The Letter Then Write Your Own.

Trace The Letter Then Write Your Own.

F F F F F F F F F F F

f f f f f f f f f f f f f f f f

Trace The Letter Then Write Your Own.

Trace The Letter Then Write Your Own.

Trace The Letter Then Write Your Own.

Trace The Letter Then Write Your Own.

Trace The Letter Then Write Your Own.

K K K K K K K K K

k k k k k k k k k k k

Trace The Letter Then Write Your Own.

Trace The Letter Then Write Your Own.

Trace The Letter Then Write Your Own.

Trace The Letter Then Write Your Own.

Trace The Letter Then Write Your Own.

Trace The Letter Then Write Your Own.

Trace The Letter Then Write Your Own.

Trace The Letter Then Write Your Own.

Trace The Letter Then Write Your Own.

Trace The Letter Then Write Your Own.

Trace The Letter Then Write Your Own.

V V V V V V V V V V

v v v v v v v v v v

Trace The Letter Then Write Your Own.

Trace The Letter Then Write Your Own.

Trace The Letter Then Write Your Own.

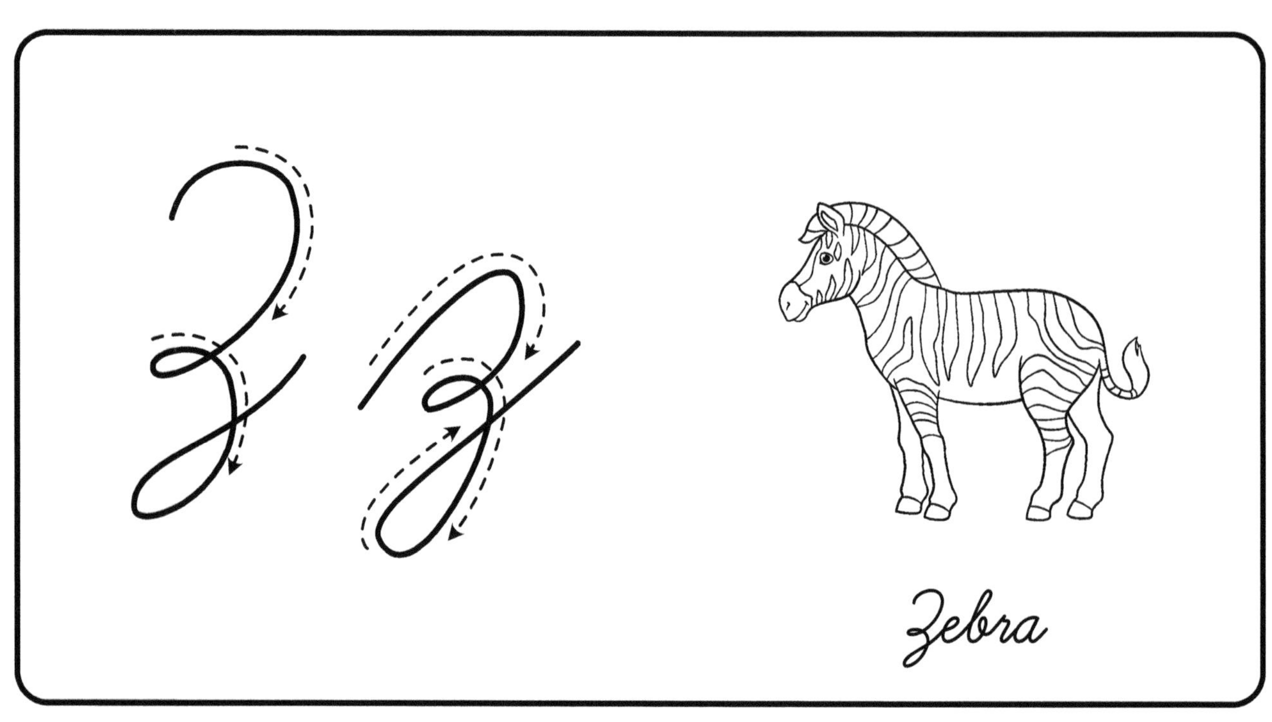

Trace The Letter Then Write Your Own.

Trace The Number Then Write Your Own.

1 1 1 1 1 1 1 1 1 1 1 1 1 1

One One One One One

Two

Trace The Number Then Write Your Own.

2 2 2 2 2 2 2 2 2 2 2 2

Two Two Two Two Two

Trace The Number Then Write Your Own.

3 3 3 3 3 3 3 3 3 3 3 3

Three Three Three Three

Trace The Number Then Write Your Own.

4 4 4 4 4 4 4 4 4 4 4

Four Four Four Four

Trace The Number Then Write Your Own.

5 5 5 5 5 5 5 5 5 5 5 5

Five Five Five Five

Trace The Number Then Write Your Own.

6 6 6 6 6 6 6 6 6 6 6 6

Six Six Six Six Six

Trace The Number Then Write Your Own.

7 7 7 7 7 7 7 7 7 7 7 7

Seven Seven Seven

Trace The Number Then Write Your Own.

8 8 8 8 8 8 8 8 8 8 8

Eight Eight Eight Eight

Trace The Number Then Write Your Own.

9 9 9 9 9 9 9 9 9 9 9

Nine Nine Nine Nine

10
Ten
Trace The Number Then Write Your Own.
10 10 10 10 10 10 10 10
Ten Ten Ten Ten Ten Ten

Trace The Words Then Write Your Own.
Apple Apple Apple Apple
Apple Apple Apple Apple
Apple Apple Apple Apple

Trace The Words Then Write Your Own.

Bear Bear Bear Bear

Bear Bear Bear Bear

Bear Bear Bear Bear

Trace The Words Then Write Your Own.
Cat Cat Cat Cat Cat
Cat Cat Cat Cat Cat
Cat Cat Cat Cat Cat

Trace The Words Then Write Your Own.

Dog Dog Dog Dog Dog

Dog Dog Dog Dog Dog

Dog Dog Dog Dog Dog

Trace The Words Then Write Your Own.

Trace The Words Then Write Your Own.

Frog Frog Frog Frog

Frog Frog Frog Frog

Frog Frog Frog Frog

Trace The Words Then Write Your Own.
Gorilla Gorilla Gorilla
Gorilla Gorilla Gorilla
Gorilla Gorilla Gorilla

Trace The Words Then Write Your Own.

Hat Hat Hat Hat Hat

Hat Hat Hat Hat Hat

Hat Hat Hat Hat Hat

Trace The Words Then Write Your Own.
Ice cream Ice cream
Ice cream Ice cream
Ice cream Ice cream

Trace The Words Then Write Your Own.

Jump Jump Jump Jump

Jump Jump Jump Jump

Jump Jump Jump Jump

Trace The Sentence Then Write Your Own.

Adam asked Anna for

an apple.

Trace The Sentence Then Write Your Own.

Bobby bought a ball

for the baby.

Trace The Sentence Then Write Your Own.

Cecil could catch a cold.

Trace The Sentence Then Write Your Own.

Dessie decides on a delicious

dessert.

Trace The Sentence Then Write Your Own.

Ellen excused herself elegantly.

Trace The Sentence Then Write Your Own.

Frank found a funny fort.

Trace The Sentence Then Write Your Own.

Ginger gave George some geese.

Trace The Sentence Then Write Your Own.

Hannah has a happy house.

Trace The Sentence Then Write Your Own.

Ivan's idea is intelligent.

Trace The Sentence Then Write Your Own.

June's jewelry jingles.

www.ingramcontent.com/pod-product-compliance
Ingram Content Group UK Ltd.
Pitfield, Milton Keynes, MK11 3LW, UK
UKHW051133260726
13967UKWH00010B/3016

9 780578 925745